YOUR KNOWLEDGE HAS VALUE

- We will publish your bachelor's and master's thesis, essays and papers

- Your own eBook and book - sold worldwide in all relevant shops

- Earn money with each sale

Upload your text at www.GRIN.com and publish for free

Melanie Anders

"Chicano English" and "Türkendeutsch": A comparison of two ethnic dialects

GRIN Verlag

Bibliografische Information der Deutschen Nationalbibliothek:

Die Deutsche Bibliothek verzeichnet diese Publikation in der Deutschen National-
bibliografie; detaillierte bibliografische Daten sind im Internet über http://dnb.d-
nb.de/ abrufbar.

Imprint:

Copyright © 2012 GRIN Verlag GmbH
Druck und Bindung: Books on Demand GmbH, Norderstedt Germany
ISBN: 978-3-656-36330-9

This book at GRIN:

http://www.grin.com/en/e-book/208515/chicano-english-and-tuerkendeutsch-a-
comparison-of-two-ethnic-dialects

Bayerische Julius – Maximilians – Universität Würzburg
Neuphilologisches Institut
Lehrstuhl für Anglistik/ Amerikanistik

"American English: History, Variation, and Change"
Wintersemester 2011

Chicano English and Türkendeutsch –
A comparison of two ethnic dialects

10.02.2012

Melanie Anders

LA Gymnasium Deutsch/ Englisch
9./ 8. Semester

Table of contents

1. Introduction

In every living language, processes of change are as inevitable as rain.[1]

New dialects develop out of isolation as well as out of contact with other varieties. Thereby they are influenced by ongoing socio-cultural changes and, in turn, affect culture and way of speaking. This paper will summarize results of latest linguistic research on two ethnic dialects – Chicano English, a Hispanic variety of American English and Türkendeutsch[2], a relatively new variety of German. First, both varieties will be presented with regard to their history, their structural features and sociolinguistic aspects, starting with Chicano English. After outlining characteristics of both individually, major similarities and differences will be highlighted. Finally, difficulties in the context of this paper will be discussed and future prospects will be given.

2. Chicano English

As Carmen Fought points out in her treatise *Chicano English in context* there are still some persistent myths and misconceptions about what Chicano English actually is and who it speaks. In this chapter, Chicano English (CE) will be defined as regards its historical background, its structural properties as well as sociolinguistic aspects.

Chicano English is a very wide-spread Hispanic variety of American English spoken in California and other south-western states of the USA. It is a non-standard ethnic dialect with low prestige and is often mistaken for English with a Spanish accent or an erroneous English of speakers whose mother tongue is Spanish. In fact, it is the vernacular of millions of native Californian English speakers many of whom cannot even speak Spanish. Although CE might sound Hispanic to a certain extent, due to its Mexican roots, it is still an independent local dialect with typical patterns and rules and people of all ages, social classes and occupational backgrounds speak it.

2.1 The History of Chicano English

Just as other dialects, Chicano English grew out of language contact. California, especially Los Angeles, has always been a multilingual and multicultural melting pot with today's largest Hispanic community.

---

[1] (Field 2011: 109)
[2] Turkish – German

The predecessor of CE evolved out of bilingualism. English and Spanish speakers came into contact with each other not least because of trade between Mexico and the US. Until the Mexican – American war in 1848 California was a part of Mexico. More and more Anglos settled in Mexican territory trying to dominate the region. During the Mexican – American war in 1848 US forces occupied major Mexican cities. With the defeat of the Mexican army the US gained one third of Mexican territory. Even though English became the primary language of government, education and economy as well as the second language for many Mexicans, Spanish-influenced varieties of English have existed since in the southwest. Succeeding generations of early Mexican immigrants grew up bilingual and shaped the dialect of those regions.

2.2 Structural features of Chicano English

CE is an independent dialect with its own structural features. In the following, typical characteristics of Chicano English will be presented.

2.2.1 Prosody and Intonation

Undoubtedly the Mexican Spanish influx is still present in today's Chicano English. The most salient hints are to be found in the intonation and the prosody. Other than in standard American English with a rise – fall (2-3-1) intonation pattern for declarative sentences, CE speakers start utterances with a higher pitch and don't end as abrupt as in (3-2…-) 4-3 (Fought 2003: 73). This "circumflex"[3] intonation has its origin in Mexican Spanish. Within this pattern statements sound like questions. Even though this is also true for the local Californian *uptalk* CE still differs from it as it features even higher pitches. Older CE speakers use the "circumflex" intonation pattern more often than younger ones who also use *uptalk* occasionally. In addition, high pitched talk is often heard in the media where Mexican and Chicano speech patterns are ridiculed.

The rhythm and melody of CE speakers' utterances are also distinct from those of other English varieties. While English is a stress timed language, Spanish is syllable timed. In terms of stress CE holds an intermediate position between English and Spanish. Stresses in CE are often placed within a word as in the compound *morning sickness* where stresses are on *{mor}* and *{sick}* (Fought 2003: 71). So there are two strong stresses rather than one main stress within one word. In combinations of verb plus particle as in *to sit up* (Fought 2003: 71)

---

[3] Fought (2003: 73) refers to Matluck who was the first to describe this kind of intonation as "circumflex"

the stress is more likely to be on the verb *sit* unlike in other English dialects where the particle *up* would be stressed.

Finally, there are two characteristic suprasegmental features of Chicano English. One is the phenomenon of *creaky voice*, which CE incorporated from the local Anglo dialect, where it is very popular especially among women. Some of them end almost every sentence with a creak in their voice. The other concerns *clicks*.[4] Those are mainly articulated by male gang members and serve as discourse markers that mostly express disapproval.

2.2.2 Phonology

Other salient characteristics of CE are to be found in its phonology. In unstressed syllables CE speakers reduce vowels, especially high vowels like /i/ or /u/, less frequently than speakers of the local Anglo dialect. Hence, a CE speaker would pronounce *together* like [tʰugɛðɚ] (Fought 2003: 64) in contrast to [tʰə'geðər] of Anglo speakers. Furthermore there is a frequent lack of glides in CE pronunciation as for example in *ago* [əgo] vs. Standard American English [ə'goʊ]. In CE the phoneme /ɪ/ occurs as tense /i:/ in words like *embarrassing* [ɪmbɛrəsin] (Fought 2003: 65). Generally speaking, vowels in CE are articulated slightly higher. Not only are there differences in the articulation of vowels, in CE consonants are also replaced or reduced. The alveolar plosives /t/ and /d/ substitute the dental fricatives /ð/ and /θ/, a feature which is known to occur in African American English as well. There is consonant cluster reduction in the form of /t/ or /d/ deletion at the end of words as in *least* [lis], *night* [naj] or even within words as in *hardware* [hɑwɚ] (Fought 2003: 68-9). CE speakers tend to glottalise final voiceless stops or aspirate them.

2.2.3 Syntax and Semantics of Chicano English

Chicano English shares many syntactical features with other non – standard varieties. Those include the use of negative concord, an alteration of *was/ were* and a lack of agreement in 3rd person singular forms. There is regularization of past tense and irregular verb forms as well as the usage of *ain't*. Features that derive from contact with African American Vernacular English (AAVE) such as invariant *be*, existential *it* and perfective *had* can also be found in Chicano English. But what is typical for CE only is on the one hand the use of the modal *would* in if – clauses for example in *If he'd be here right now, he'd make me laugh* (Fought 2003: 99) and on the other hand preposition substitution as in *We all make mistakes*

---

[4] An alveolar or palato-alveolar sound, its IPA symbol is /ǃ/

along life (Fought 2003: 101). In both cases Spanish constructions might have reinforced the CE usage. Bilinguals or early speakers of CE might have simply drawn an analogy between the Spanish and the English patterns, as the syntax of both languages is fairly similar. The modal *could* in the meaning of "can/ to have the competence to do sth." as in *Nobody believes that you could fix anything* (Fought 2003: 100) is frequently used by CE speakers but is not to be found in any other non – standard variety or rather among Anglo speakers.

In terms of lexicon CE consists of much informal slang and colloquial expressions for example *fool* meaning "guy" or *talk to* for "to date sb." (Fought 2003: 103), those are mainly used by young speakers. Some expressions have their source in Spanish for example *barely* in the sense of "just recently" or the Mexican Spanish discourse marker *ey* (Fought 2003: 104). Because of a growing Chicano – Literature and an upcoming Latino discourse more and more Mexican Spanish words for food (*tortilla, burrito…*) and Mexican cultural items find their way into Chicano English (Field 2011: 128).

With regard to the Mexican Spanish influence on syntactical and phonological features and in particular on pronunciation it is hardly surprising that CE speakers are mistaken for native Spanish speakers so often. However, beside the dialectal features, speakers use certain linguistic features intentionally to establish their identities as will be shown in the following.

2.3 Sociolinguistic aspects of Chicano English

Language is one of the most important means to express identity. On the one hand, speakers establish their identity through language by using certain features intentionally. On the other hand, they deduce certain social and cultural circumstances from a way of speaking. As CE is an ethnic minority dialect with low prestige, there a many prejudices against its speakers and some of them are still discriminated at work, in schools or on the street. Many preconceptions are based on the assumption that CE speakers are gang affiliated. In fact, the gang status does influence the use of linguistic features even more than the social status does.

In her study, Fought investigated the phonetic variation of her speakers on a sociolinguistic basis and with regard to gender, social class and gang status. For one thing she found out that minority communities do take part in sound changes of the local majority variety. Such contemporary sound changes in the Californian Anglo community are /u/ - fronting, /æ/ - backing and raising. For another thing she addressed social circumstances under which speakers use these features.

The construction of identity is complex and constituted by many factors such as age, gender, socioeconomic background and subcultural aspects like gang membership. It also depends on social role models and gender norms. In the Latino community girls are supposed to be feminine and compliant, boys have to be strong and tough. Toughness again is also associated with gang membership as well as working class belonging whereas the middle class status is linked to conservatism. In general, /u/ - fronting in CE is very common among working class women with no gang affiliation and could be a sign of social assimilation; however there are female middle class gang members who front their /u/. Backing of /æ/ is also more common among women and non gang members. Male non gang members from the working class raise their /æ/ almost as frequent as male middle class gang members. Fought explains that speakers with complex identities such as female middle class gang members who combine opposing social concepts of toughness, conservatism and femininity use those linguistic features more frequently to express their gender roles. Here, the identity aspect "gender" is more important for speakers than their gang membership or social status. Homogeneous groups such as working class gang members show less gender variation in their use of /u/ - fronting, /æ/ - backing and raising.

Generally, non-gang members reject features gang speakers use. However, speakers who identify with gang image use gang speech features even more. Taggers[5], for example, use negative concord most frequently in order to sound tougher and more like actual gang members. Here, certain phonological and syntactical features are used intentionally in order to establish an image, an identity and highlight how speakers want to be seen.

3. Türkendeutsch

3.1 The emergence of Türkendeutsch

This ethnic variety of German which is also referred to as *Kanakisch*[6] or *Türkenslang* is a relatively new phenomenon. It originates in large German cities like Frankfurt, Berlin or Hamburg which became multilingual and multicultural melting pots ever since the late 20th century. Initially, during the 1990's, Türkendeutsch was a new ethnolect, even ghetto slang spoken by young, male 2. or 3. generation immigrants whose parents came to Germany as

---

[5] Taggers "[…] they are completely separate from the gang members […] often are adolescents who have moved to the area more recently. […] The term comes from tagging, the practice of writing graffiti […] Taggers focus their energy on this activity, rather than on more violent ones." (Fought 2003: 51)

[6] Dago; The term derives from *Kanake*, a pejorative term for Turkish immigrant workers or people with southern European look in general

5

"Gastarbeiter"[7]. These youths of southern European or Arabic descent tried to distance themselves from their parents' generation as well as from German society and therefore created their own speech style which spread quickly even among non-Turkish-born speakers.

Beginning in 1995, the new ethnolect was discussed in the German media. By imitating this speech style, successful comedy shows like "Erkan und Stefan", "Was guckst du?", and the comedy duo "Mundstuhl" addressed the new variety and its social context. The result was a "stylized"[8] version of the original ethnolect. Nationwide, particularly male adolescent speakers of German or other origin adopted features of the stylized media ethnolect. Auer (2003: 256) mentions three levels of the new ethnolect in this context. The *primary ethnolect* is mainly spoken by male German-born[9] speakers with a Turkish family background. The media, especially via comedy shows, transforms and stylizes their speech style into the *secondary ethnolect*. Thereby, salient linguistic features and typical behaviour are pointed out and ridiculed. German youths, especially male, then integrate features of the "media version" into their language which is referred to as *tertiary ethnolect*. In some cases, however, German youths acquire rather than quote the language of *primary ethnolect* speakers by direct contact and without media influence.

3.2 Structural properties of Türkendeutsch

In the following the phonological, syntactical and lexical features of the *primary ethnolect* will be presented. Additionally, features attributed to the second and third level of Türkendeutsch will be shown.

3.2.1 Phonology

One salient feature which is used consistently is the alteration of [ç] into [ʃ] as in *ich*[10] [ɪʃ]. Initially, this used to be a feature of the Central German dialect[11]. Furthermore, there is consonant cluster reduction for example /ts/ is reduced to /s/ as in *zwei* [svai][12]. Long vowels become short as in *Sohn* [zon][13]. Voiceless stops become voiced as in *Alter* [aldɐ][14]. In initial

---

[7] guest workers: due to labour shortage during the 1950's/ 1960's Western Germany concluded recruitment agreements with southern European states who sent temporary workers to Germany

[8] Deppermann uses this term

[9] They were born in Germany and might have grown up bilingual, but their mother tongue is German.

[10] I

[11] Including vernaculars of West and East Central German spoken in Saarland, Rhineland, Hesse, Thuringia, Saxony

[12] two

[13] son

[14] buddy

sound clusters /r/ is often pronounced apically. Glottal stops are frequently missing. The rhythm is rather syllable-timed and said to sound jerky. According to Auer (2003: 258), these characteristics can be clearly traced back to Turkish influx.

3.2.2 Syntax and semantics

Turkish is an agglutinating language which has neither gender nor articles. There are no prepositions; agreement of gender, number and case does not exist. The general sentence structure in Turkish is *subject – object – verb*. These characteristics reappear in the *primary ethnolect* described by Auer (2003: 258/59). Türkendeutsch speakers seem to change the gender of words impromptu. In terms of agreement there are many errors as in *einer Deutscher* (vs. *ein Deutscher*) [15]. Articles are often left out for example in *Gibt Problem? (vs. Gibt es ein Problem?)* [16] or in *gehmer Tankstelle (vs. gehmer an die Tankstelle)* [17] where both preposition *an* and article *die* are missing. In addition, pronouns are left out frequently as well as in *als ich kennengelernt hab* (vs. *als ich sie kennengelernt hab*) [18]. There are also errors in word order and sentence structure. Discourse markers like *h(ey)* or *Alter* and intensifiers such as *krass* [19] or *korrekt* [20] are very common together with set phrases like *ich schwör* [21] (Kern 2008: 309).

3.2.3 Features of stylized Türkendeutsch

Speakers of the *secondary* and *tertiary ethnolect* use all the characteristics mentioned above and even add or overuse certain features. Comedians, for example, use a retroflex [R] almost exclusively. Speakers in Deppermanns study used the ü-umlaut /y/ and shifted vowels as in *ey* [œɪ] instead of [ɛɪ] to imply Turkish pronunciation. Turkish words like *lan, tam, çog iyi* [22] (Deppermann 2007: 57) and tags like *verstehsdu* [23] (Auer 2003: 256) are incorporated. The use of the article and pronoun *dem/den* [24] is overgeneralized. Altogether the *secondary ethnolect* is an exaggerated and compressed version of the primary variant.

---

[15] A German; the speaker might have drawn an analogy to the ending –*er* in *Deutscher* and simply added this inflectional ending to *ein,* so that both words have the same ending
[16] Is there (a) problem? The indefinite article *ein* is missing as well as the pronoun *es* that belongs to the verb
[17] We go to the gas station – *gehmer* is a contraction of *gehen* (to go) and *mer* (as allomorph of *wir* - we)
[18] When I (have) met her; *hab* is colloquial for *habe* (I have)
[19] Extremely, great, strange
[20] Exactly, right, correct
[21] I swear, No kidding! As in Turkish *Vallah*
[22] buddy, exactly, okay/very good
[23] Do you understand? *Verstehsdu* is a contraction of *verstehst* (to understand) and *du* (you) – 2. person singular interrogative form; due to consonant cluster reduction the /t/ has been deleted
[24] the; *den* (the accusative from of the masculine article *der*) is used in every case

3.3 Sociolinguistic aspects

As already mentioned, Türkendeutsch is a new ethnic variety spoken by mainly male native German youths with or without Turkish background. Speakers of this "ethnic style" (Kern 2008: 309) know and are perfectly able to produce standard German. Türkendeutsch is used intentionally, as a part of a speakers' repertoire, and in informal conversations for various reasons. It is a form of code switching/ language crossing and not a result of an erroneous second language acquisition.

Primary ethnolect speakers use it in order to express ethnicity and to refer ironically to the faulty German of their parents and grandparents' generation. The media imitates their speech style for entertainment reasons, creates stereotypes and thereby responds to the challenges of a multicultural society.

According to Depperman (2007: 47-58), stylized Türkendeutsch is used in only three different conversation situations. Firstly, when quoting a person of the *primary ethnolect*, speakers perform a code switch and increasingly use retroflex [R], voiced [t] and code markers like *krass* or *alder*. Thereby they position and distance themselves from speakers of the *primary ethnolect* whose language they regard as less intelligent. Here, stylized Türkendeutsch serves as a means of mockery and irony. Secondly, in order to caricature the *primary ethnolect* speakers and their image and thereby gain the laughs of the listeners, speakers of stylized Türkendeutsch use category bound features[25] like the ü-umlaut, jerky rhythm and threats. Other than *secondary ethnolect* speakers they don't quote a *primary ethnolect* speaker but rather create a language which they find indicative for this group of speakers. Thirdly, the *tertiary ethnolect* is used most frequently in peer-group internal rhetoric contest. The imitation of the *primary ethnolect* is accompanied by extreme evaluations that are typical for youth language and peer group interaction. By repeating and completing code markers youths outdo each other and get each other worked up. He who can produce a code which is the furthest away from standard wins this "poetic" competition. Again, the code switch serves amusement and entertainment.

Even though Türkendeutsch has low prestige, is constantly mocked and a breeding ground for irony, it still gives *tertiary speakers* a chance to individuate, to establish a sense of unity in their peer groups and is not least a forum for speakers to demonstrate their knowledge of current media shows as well as their observation and rhetoric skills.

---

[25] Ways of speaking that are indicative for a certain social category or group

4. Similarities and differences of both varieties

Both ethnic dialects are relatively young phenomena and developed out of language contact especially in large multicultural cities. Speakers of both varieties are natives and master the standard language. Often they are mistaken for second language learners with a strong accent. But while CE is a nationwide dialect spoken by people of all ages, gender and occupation as their mother tongue, Türkendeutsch is rather slang, a style, youth language used intentionally and in certain conversation situations by mainly male speakers. Hence, Türkendeutsch is only a part of a speakers' repertoire, an additional means of expression and is, according to Deppermann, particularly used in comical contexts.

Traces of their original contact language can still be found in the lexis, syntax and phonology of both varieties. Based on the source language, prepositions are either changed as in CE or left out as in Türkendeutsch. Discourse markers are used frequently as well as single words of the source language. Both varieties borrowed syntactical features with the result that some constructions would be regarded incorrect in standard language. CE, for example, uses *would* in if-clauses, Türkendeutsch alters the sentence structure. Other syntactic errors in Türkendeutsch are frequent and desired for category establishing reasons. With regard to phonology, both dialects feature consonant cluster reduction in form of /t/ deletion. Vowels in CE are pronounced higher and longer, whereas Türkendeutsch speakers tend to articulate them shorter. In terms of prosody, both varieties feature a syllable timed rhythm and stress patterns different from their local standard variety.

5. Conclusion

In the course of this paper, two ethnic dialects – Türkendeutsch and Chicano English – have been discussed and compared as regards the structural and sociolinguistic aspects. As for the topic of Türkendeutsch, it wasn't easy to find applicable profound specialist literature. More empirical research needs to be done on this phenomenon especially in respect of female speakers. Undoubtedly, by now, Türkendeutsch has spread even further and is now used by female speakers as well and in more contexts. Today, not only comedy shows refer to this way of speaking but also many famous German Hip Hop singers. One could argue that the growing German Hip Hop culture influences the youth and their speech as well as their attitude even stronger than TV comedy shows do. Furthermore, it is easily conceivable that features of Türkendeutsch will make it into standard German soon.

Regarding Chicano English, one can only hope that the prejudices against CE speakers will finally disappear and a greater awareness for linguistic individuality will evolve among speakers of majority varieties. Hence, future studies could investigate how CE speakers are portrayed in the media or which associations they evoke in non – CE speakers.

Language should be something to be proud of, not something to get discriminated for.

Bibliography

Auer, Peter. 2003. ",Türkenslang': Ein jugendsprachlicher Ethnolekt des Deutschen und seine Transformationen" In *Spracherwerb und Lebensalter*, Annelies Häcki Buhofer (ed), 255 – 264. Tübingen: Francke.

Deppermann, Arnulf. 2007. "Stilisiertes Türkendeutsch in Gesprächen deutscher Jugendlicher. " *Zeitschrift für Literaturwissenschaft und Linguistik* 37 (148): 43-62.

Field, Frederic. 2011. *Bilingualism in the USA. The case of the Chicano – Latino community.* Amsterdam/ Philadelphia: John Benjamins.

Fought, Carmen. 2003. *Chicano English in Context.* New York: Palgrave.

Häcki Buhofer, Annelies. 2003. *Spracherwerb und Lebensalter.* Tübingen: Francke.

Kern, Friederike. 2008. "Türkendeutsch. Ein ethnischer Sprachstil." In *Die Sprache Deutsch: eine Ausstellung des Deutschen Historischen Museums Berlin [15. Januar 2009 bis 3. Mai 2009]*, Heidemarie Anderlik (ed), 309-310. Dresden: Sandstein.

http://articles.latimes.com/print/2011/oct/24/local/la-me-eastla-accent-20111025

http://jannisandroutsopoulos.files.wordpress.com/2009/12/ds-4-2001.pdf

http://www.verlag-gespraechsforschung.de/2006/pdf/gui-kern.pdf

http://home.edo.uni-dortmund.de/~hoffmann/ABC/Tuerkisch.html

http://en.wikipedia.org/wiki/Central_German

http://de.wikipedia.org/wiki/T%C3%BCrkische_Sprache